T0380450

LIFE—Living Intentionally, Forever Emerging

Michelle Jones

AuthorHouse™ UK
1663 Liberty Drive
Bloomington, IN 47403 USA
www.authorhouse.co.uk
Phone: 0800 047 8203 (Domestic TFN)
+44 1908 723714 (International)

Published by AuthorHouse 08/01/2019

ISBN: 978-1-7283-9129-8 (sc)
ISBN: 978-1-7283-9128-1 (e)

Print information available on the last page.

This book is printed on acid-free paper.

authorHOUSE®

First and foremost, to my heavenly Father, who entrusted me with His vision. Thank You. I hope I've done You proud.

I would like to thank every woman who has survived. Your determination and resilience to win, whilst clothed with grace, class, and strength cannot be defined. The lemons life has thrown at you, has produced the world's finest lemonade.

ABOUT THE AUTHOR

Naturally encouraging and compassionate as a child, Michelle was always drawn to befriend the 'unpopular' children at school. In hindsight, she now realises that this was her gift. She had, and still has, the ability to see past her own issues with a passion to help others.

Though life will have challenges, Michelle believes that there are solutions to every situation. She believes that the answers are all in the Word of God. It was whilst Michelle worked in the corporate sector, that she realised her gift. She had the ability to coach, mentor, and motivate her staff members effortlessly. This produced tangible results, as her employees who had previously been unsuccessful received promotions.

Michelle has also worked with women who have survived physical, emotional, and psychological abuse. This is where she witnessed first-hand the damaging after-effects of abuse, and the impact it had on lives.

Another pivotal point in Michelle's life happened whilst she was working in the field of housing. She met with a resident who was extremely concerned about her son, but was unable to articulate what was wrong with him. All she would say was that he spent most of his time in bed, and wouldn't leave his room. Alarm bells began to ring at this point. Especially because, on that particular bright and sunny day, late in the afternoon, the residents son was still in bed, the lights were on, and the curtains drawn. With the resident's permission, Michelle spoke to her son. Drawing from her experience, she recognised that he was showing signs of depression. After spending approximately thirty minutes with him, she managed to gain his trust, educate him about depression, remove the stigma and sign-posted him to his Doctor. She doesn't remember what she said verbatim, but remembers feeling a significant shift in the trajectory of her life in that moment.

When she visited two weeks later, she had learned that the young man, after not having left his home for two years, had got himself a part-time job. Michelle had found what she had been looking for all of her life—her calling.

As an accredited coach and mentor, Michelle specialises in resilience and confidence coaching. She is also a qualified Mental Health First Aider.

Michelle's passion is to reignite the purpose and hope that she believes every woman carries. She is a firm believer that age is nothing but a number, and that it is never too late to start.

CONTENTS

INTRODUCTION

Before we go any further, I want you to say with meaning, 'This is going to be the best year of my life!'

It may often take a wake-up call to raise our awareness and provoke the realisation, that we are in need and want of change. Living with trauma, depression, anxiety, or low self-esteem can often leave many of us feeling frustrated and confused about the purpose of life. These feelings can become overwhelming. As a society, we have become very good at concealing hurt and trauma, caused by the stigma and shame associated with mental health illnesses. Although low self-esteem isn't regarded as a mental illness, it can certainly attribute to it. Low self-esteem can cause us to make wrong choices, tolerate things we shouldn't, and settle for less. In Proverbs 13:12, we read, 'Hope deferred makes the heart sick.' When hope, expectation and vision is delayed, we become sick in our hearts and minds.

Depression and anxiety can still be taboo subjects within some Christian communities. There are many 'mask-wearing' Christians pretending to be content and fulfilled with life. The truth is, internally they have lost hope and are merely existing. If that's you, it's time to take the mask off, it's time to be open and transparent about your struggles. Low self-esteem, depression, and anxiety do not care about your social status, religious views, or economic position. They are thieves, their jobs are to steal, kill, and destroy. There is good news though; in John 10:10, we learn that Jesus came so that *you* may have and enjoy life—and have it in abundance. This means to the fullest, until it overflows. Doesn't that fill you with hope?

Answering truthfully, can you say that any of the following apply to you?

- Feeling inferior
- Feeling less worthy
- Overly suspicious
- Unbalanced negative perception
- Co-dependent

- Hypersensitive
- Self-critical
- Constantly striving for perfection
- Focusing on what others think of you
- Struggle in relationships

This list is not exhaustive. If you are living with depression, anxiety, or low self-esteem, it's extremely likely that you have experienced living with some of these feelings.

I want you to congratulate yourself for being brave enough to even 'go there', it isn't easy, so well done for raising your awareness. These feelings are just protective mechanisms that you have subconsciously built up and put in place over the years. Many people have become fearful and paralysed by low self-esteem, they perceive life from a negative viewpoint, this can be an extremely exhausting way to live.

We have seen how social media can have a detrimental impact on those already feeling isolated and lonely. It's often when we are feeling low that we succumb to the urge of comparing our lives to the lives of others. Social media has depleted in many of us, the art of being relational with one another. It can also be extremely misleading, especially because most of what we see is not a true reflection of what is really happening. Be mindful and manage your usage responsibly.

I have no doubt that any form of trauma will bring change to your life. The question is, will that change be positive or negative? You are the only person who has the power to make that decision. The fractures and scars on our hearts, minds and souls are invisible. It is because of this, that we often trivialise the importance of this healing process. What would happen if you continued to use a fractured bone without the appropriate support? There are many people living without the diagnosis of depression or anxiety, yet they have managed to exist in the best ways they know how to. But it doesn't have to be that way. Often, it's not until you realise where you are in life, that you recognise, you have been living not by design but by default. It's time to take stock of where you currently are, and implement changes for effective, intentional outcomes.

There are thousands living with depression and anxiety, living with conditions such as agoraphobia (a fear of having a panic attack whilst out in open or crowded places), or social anxiety (feeling negatively perceived or not accepted in social settings). These issues are very common but are rarely discussed. In my opinion, one of the main contributing factors to anxiety is 'mind chatter'—you know, that voice we don't consciously hear, but it's speaking from our subconscious mind. This continuous internal dialogue in autopilot, solidifies and reinforces fear. Job 3:25 reads, 'What I always feared has happened to me; what I dreaded has come true.' Our behaviours and thoughts are self-fulfilling; what we project is what we get back. Guess what? *You* can short-circuit and rewire that negative narrative! Raising your awareness and becoming mindful of your internal dialogue will give you an advantage. You will be able to regain your power and reprogram the script being played out in your mind. Consistency, positivity and resilience, will bring the life changing results you have longed for. Remember, life is about choice. You are in control of what you can control, continually remind yourself: 'This is a process. I will take one step at a time.' You'll be well on your way!

The first step is acknowledging that you want and need help. The second is to believe that God is your loving Father, waiting to help you. Cry out to Him. The third, and certainly not the least, is to seek medical intervention and therapy if you feel that is what you need.

I quote the late Maya Angelou, who wrote, 'If you don't like something, change it, if you can't change it, change your attitude.' Change is a choice. The actions and declarations in this book are intentionally basic; their objectives are to get you moving, feeling, and thinking.

My intention is in no way to take the Word of God out of context; instead, I encourage you to read the Bible in its entirety. You have the authority and power, through the Word of God, to defeat anything that opposes your God-given inheritance, to be free and live abundantly. You really are not alone on this journey. If you are not a Christian woman; but can identify with some of the points raised, I believe there is something in this book for you.

Congratulations and well done for making this decision.

CHAPTER 1

Gratitude

Have there been times when you have felt low, unfulfilled, or hopeless for what appears to be no apparent reason? Have there been times when you have been overcome by self-pity and have just been unable to see that anything in your life was working out? There were times in my own life when I experienced these feelings. I couldn't always find the trigger, but I was aware that my subconscious mind was playing out negative thoughts. I would get caught up in a spiral of thoughts, thinking about what I didn't have and what I hadn't achieved, rather than what I *did* have, and what I *had* achieved. It was so easy to get caught up in this mindset, and sometimes hard to shake off.

If you can relate to this, I've got some good news: I have found a powerful antidote to counteract these feelings. It's simply to praise and thank God for what I *do* have. Hebrews 13:15 tells us that we should continually offer the sacrifice of praise to God. I believe that praise is even more effective and powerful when it is unprompted. When you begin to focus on what God is doing and has done in your life, something magical happens—a fountain of gratitude will begin to overflow inside of you. You'll begin to feel overwhelmed by a renewed great appreciation for life. You'll experience joy in great depth; you'll feel a supernatural surge of strength, hopefulness, and excitement, amongst many other emotions. This is not just a feeling or emotion. It's a recharge of your spirit, because you are connected to the Source.

The next time you begin to feel *those* feelings, focus on the fact that:

- You've opened your eyes this morning.
- You are healthy, and you are in your right mind.
- You've heard birds singing.
- You've felt the elements on your skin.

Make a decision to be intentional about being happy, to be in the present moment, and to appreciate all that you have. Sure, you may not be where you want to be right now. You may not have all that you want. As bleak as your situation may seem, there is somebody out there who would love to trade places with you in a heartbeat. You are blessed. What are you grateful for today? Set aside at least 30 minutes for the next 30 days, to praise and thank God. The fact that today wasn't promised and you are here, is a good reason to start.

CHAPTER 2

Limiting Beliefs!

Do you often find yourself wanting to achieve more in life but are constantly reminded by your subconscious mind that you can't do it—perhaps because of your age, your gender, your education, your race, or your disability?

Do you find yourself saying things like, 'Life is hard', 'I won't be able to do this', or 'I'm not good enough'? These are your beliefs; they are dream-limiting killers. They have robbed many people of their destinies. A vast amount of women have struggled with this mindset at some point in their lives. Unfortunately, many women have become immune to this negative internal dialogue, because they have lived with it throughout their whole lives. They have become desensitised by it. These beliefs are the main obstacles that prevent you from achieving your goals. If you don't acknowledge them, you will be forever imprisoned and stagnant. Your beliefs have been shaped and influenced by your childhood, your environment, and your past experiences. This is what you have been taught to believe. These thought patterns have been handed down through generations. Your beliefs are being played out in the movie called *Real Life*, starring none other than *you*.

The great news is that the Word of God has given us instructions to deal with this. For example, in 2 Corinthians 10:5, we have been given the authority to 'cast down imaginations, and every high thing that exalts itself against the knowledge of God, bringing into captivity every thought to the obedience of Christ'. For many of us, the 'abnormal', according to God's standards, has become normal. If you want to change, you must first destroy these limiting thoughts. I must warn you though, limitation does not like change. They are bad habits that need to be broken, they will challenge you. But you must keep going. You have been given a spirit of power, love, and a sound mind. Remember your tongue is the ready writer and has the power of death and life in it. Create laws that give life. Always have this thought in mind: A belief is an acceptance that a statement is true or that something exists, especially without proof. The next time you hear that limiting belief, ask, what evidence is there that this is true?

Friendships

CHAPTER 3

Friendships

For many women, the art of making and maintaining friendships is easy, it's not given a second thought. There are women who suffer from social anxiety disorders, and so this seemingly natural thing to do can be extremely difficult. If you've never struggled in this area, you may not fully comprehend the effects of anxiety. The fact is, there are many lonely and isolated people in the world. Loneliness is cruel, painful, and selfish. There are many people who do not feel worthy of having friendships. This is normally a reflection of how they see themselves—their self-esteem.

To be a good friend, you need to first start off liking and loving yourself. Your relationship with yourself is second only to your relationship with God. You can teach yourself how to be intentional about cultivating and valuing your friendships and relationships. Interestingly, the dictionary defines 'friendship' as the 'relationship' between friends, so the two go hand in hand.

The next time you get the opportunity, observe how young children interact with one another. We can learn so much from them. They're non-judgemental, they don't overthink or overcomplicate the art of making friends. By their actions, we can see that it's obvious that we are created as interdependent, social beings. We don't function well in isolation. Healthy relationships don't just happen, we need to play our part.

It's time to take inventory of your inner circle. The Bible tells us that iron sharpens iron. Who you have around you is important. Stop settling for people who consistently undermine your boundaries and do not respect you. This chapter will empower you to take responsibility for your relationships.

'Not giving up meeting together, as some are in the habit of doing, but encouraging one another—and all the more as you see the day approaching' (Hebrews 10:25 NIV).

Action you can take—Conversation: Invite some friends and/or family members over to your place. As the host, choose the theme or topic for the evening. On small pieces of paper, write meaningful statements or questions relating to your theme. Place the pieces of paper in a jar. In turn, ask your guests to select a piece of paper. Ask them to respond to the question/statement accordingly. The aim is to provoke discussion and/or debate.

Wise counsel: We are social, relational beings. God Himself said that it is not good for humans to be alone. I do not believe that He was referring only to marriage. We can only truly be interdependent when we are independent, so working on yourself and being the best version of you will help you become a better friend.

'A man that hath friends must shew himself friendly: and there is a friend that sticketh closer than a brother' (Proverbs 18:24 KJV).

Action you can take—Stiletto Stepping: You must put yourself out there if you want to meet new people. Finding places where people have interests similar to yours is a good start. Try some of the following suggestions: Look for meetups online, search Eventbrite (an event management and ticketing website). Explore volunteer programmes. Join a book club or a gym. Take up a new hobby. Go on holidays (there are special ones for singles). Join social media groups. Enrol in educational or recreational classes. Attend church. These are only a few suggestions; can you think of anymore?

Choose one option that you will participate in, within the next 10 days. Join another activity within the next two months.

Prayer Point: Father, in the name of Jesus, teach me how to cultivate good friendships. Help me to be accommodating in love, patience and understanding. Help me to see the good in people and show me how to forgive, when I need to. Amen

'Understand this, my beloved brothers and sisters. Let everyone be quick to hear (be a careful, thoughtful listener), slow to speak (a speaker of carefully chosen words), and slow to anger (patient, reflective and forgiving).' (James 1:19 AMP)

Action you can take—Let's talk: Conversation is an art and a skill. Within the next seven days, choose and use at least one of these conversation starters—or choose your own. Start the conversation with 'Hi! How are you?' Smile, make sure your body language is open. Remember that practice makes perfect. Get used to giving your voice a platform and initiating conversations.

Conversation starters: Do you know …? Where are you from? How are you? What do you like to do in your spare time? What are your plans for the weekend?

Here are some tips: Pay someone a compliment. Listen more than you speak. Keep the conversation positive and happy. Afterwards reflect on what went well. What was awkward about the exchange? Did the conversation feel natural?

Do you know people who are great conversationalists? What observations can you make about them?

Declare: I am a confident and excellent communicator.

'Come to me, all you who are weary and burdened,
and I will give you rest' (Matthew 11:28 NIV).

Action you can take—Bon voyage: Plan a holiday, a short break, or a spa day with your friends within the next twelve months. Take the initiative and decide whether the destination will be local or international. Gather a consensus on destinations and budgets.

Wise counsel: There are *so* many obvious reasons why taking a vacation is necessary. Rest is just as important as work—even God rested on the seventh day. We need to follow His example. Time away doesn't have to be expensive or exotic—just a place where your mind, your body, and your soul can realign, rejuvenate, regroup, and rest.

*'Can two people walk together without agreeing
on the direction?'* (Amos 3:3 NLT).

Action you can take—Conflict Resolution: Complete the following sentences:

- The last time I experienced conflict was …
- I demonstrated problem-solving skills by …
- I showed understanding by …
- I demonstrated assertiveness by …
- I demonstrated active listening skills by …
- This ended as a win-win for both sides because …
- I expressed my boundaries by …

What have you learned about yourself and how you manage conflict?

Wise counsel: Conflict will always be a part of life; if there are people, there will be conflict. Many of us choose to shy away from it, but it's a character builder. Managing conflict is a skill and requires an awareness of your emotional intelligence. Conflict isn't necessarily about arguing; rather, it is about constructively managing contentious issues or disagreements. Compromise, influence, and assertiveness should all be embraced for a positive, win-win resolution.

'Give, and it will be given to you. A good measure, pressed down, shaken together and running over, will be poured into your lap. For with the measure you use, it will be measured to you. (Luke 6:38 NIV)

Action you can take—Initiate: Starting from today, take the initiative, using the following table as a guide. Be encouraged to implement your own suggestions and ideas and rotate accordingly. You got this!

In week two of the following month	Invite a friend or a few friends over to watch a movie, play board games, listen to music, chat, and relax etc.
In week three of the second month	Choose an outdoor activity to do in the daytime. In the evening (of that same day) look for an event, or go to the cinema, wine bar, restaurant, theatre etc. Do this with a friend or a group of friends.
In week one of fifth month	Invite friends on a window shopping or shopping date. Finish the day off with a meal afterwards.
In week four of eighth month	You decide

Prayer Point: Father, in the name of Jesus, I cast and bind the spirit of rejection and low self-worth. Thank You for giving me the boldness to venture into new territories. I am fearless and excited at the prospect of initiating new things. I thank You for reminding me that what I put into (anything) is what I will receive in good measure. Amen.

'Strive for peace with everyone, and for the holiness without which no one will see the Lord' (Hebrews 12:14 ESV).

Action you can take—Reflection: Create a 'friendship chart'. The idea is to keep a record of how often you have initiated contact with each friend. Show how you made contact— was it by phone, face to face, social media, and so forth. Analyse the results at the end of each month. What does this tell you?

Action you can take—Whose who: Describe your friendships and relationships. Who would you define as: your *social friends* (people you party with), *acquaintances and colleagues* (people you meet at work, church, the gym), and *loyal friends* (friends who will be there no matter what. Which category do you feel your friends would put you in?

Wise counsel: Anything of value should be cherished, maintained, and nurtured. Some relationships are like diamonds in the rough, because you are required to see past the dirt and dross, to recognise their true beauty. Relationships and friendships work the same way. The more intentional we are about them, the more we see the beauty within them and appreciate them. What are you doing to make a difference?

CHAPTER 4
Love and Value Yourself

To understand love, you need to position yourself as a daughter of the most High God, and believe that He really does love you. Learning how to acknowledge this, is vital to your perception of love and healing. His love is perfect and will cast out all fear. Everything God created was good in His sight, and that includes you. You were wonderfully and fearfully crafted as a unique masterpiece.

Unfortunately, there are many women who do not see it this way. It is often these women who exhibit a significant deficiency of self-love and self-value. How do you think God feels when you respond negatively to His creation? *You* are a reflection of Him and His handiwork. Therefore, implementing negative addendums to the prefix 'I am' is in violation of what He says about you. The idea 'if you want others to love you, you need to first love yourself' has been thrown around so much that its significance does not carry the weight and importance it deserves.

To judge and gauge healthy love, you will need to understand it. To attract the best for you, you must be the best version of you. Transitioning from relationship to relationship without healing, will result in you continually attracting the same 'type'. With the relevant intervention, you can break the cycle, recognise *'that type'* and say, 'no thank you'.

'So, where do I start?' I hear you ask. Well, what negative experiences and cruel remarks from your past are you still holding on to and believing? Was love conditional or unconditional as a child? What examples of self-love and care did you see around you in childhood? Answering these questions is a good starting point. If you really believe that you are valuable, and treat yourself in that way, others will inevitably follow suit. The acts of loving, being gentle, encouraging and rewarding yourself should be intentional. I would go as far as saying, it's essential. I believe that God wants you to refill and consistently refuel on the good things of life. Love is patient and kind as the Bible states. Learn to be these things to yourself. The objective of this chapter is to raise your awareness of self-love and value.

'You are as beautiful as Tirzah, my darling, As lovely as Jerusalem, As awesome as an army with banners' (Songs of Solomon 6:4 NASB).

Action you can take—Me Time:

- Shave your legs.
- Shape your eyebrows.
- Wash, condition, and style your hair.
- Give yourself a mani-pedi: tidy up and paint your toenails and fingernails.
- Steam, exfoliate, cleanse, tone, and moisturise your face.

Schedule in this sort of pampering for half a day, a minimum of once a month.

Wise counsel: Why are you living to work? You are your most valuable asset. Decide to be intentional about looking good. Setting aside some 'me' time is fundamental to the well-being of women. Unless you take time out for you, nobody else can or will. The main person responsible for appreciating and valuing you is *you*. 'So do you'.

'For with God nothing shall be impossible' (Luke 1:37 KJV).

Action you can take: Using the following grid as an example, each morning for the next seven days, make an assertive decision on what you choose to be, do, or say. Document the evidence that demonstrates the action you have taken.

Today I choose to …	The evidence of this is …
For example: 'Focus on the positives.'	For example: Work was stressful, but I chose to smile my way through and think positively.

Declare: I am in control of my actions. Situations don't dictate my response. I have a choice to choose.

*'She maketh herself coverings of tapestry; her clothing
is silk and purple'* (Proverbs 31:22 KJV).

Action you can take—Find your style: What is your personal style? Categorise and arrange your wardrobe by casual wear, work wear, outerwear, loungewear, nightwear, and underwear (ladies, how many matching sets do you have?). What needs to be thrown out? What do you need more of? What do you have too many of? What doesn't fit anymore? Which items complement one another? Do the same for your accessories and shoes.

Answer these questions: What do you think your clothes say about you? Do you dress intentionally? What changes (if any), would you like to make? When will you start to implement these changes?

Wise counsel: Many of us have just made do with what we wear. We are not always intentional about the way we look; instead, convenience or price dictates our choices. Just because something is reduced in price, doesn't mean it suits you! Although we do all have a style, many women don't know theirs. You can choose to be intentional about the way you look. If cost is a factor, save up for it. Aren't you worth it? Single ladies -don't wait until you are married to invest in quality underwear. Invest in yourself and start now. It's never too late to change!

*'Above all else, guard your heart, for everything
you do flows from it'* (Proverbs 4:23 NIV).

Action you can take—Declare your values: Choose ten of the following core values that reflect who you are. Feel free to add your own. Put them in order of priority. Write down what each value means to you.

Achievement, balance, challenge, community, creativity, democracy, honesty, happiness, humour, influence, inner harmony, justice, kindness, knowledge, leadership, learning, love, loyalty, openness, optimism, peace, pleasure, poise, popularity, recognition, religion, reputation, respect, responsibility, security, self-respect, service, spirituality, stability, success, status, trustworthiness, wealth, wisdom, relationships, order, pleasure, loyalty, wisdom, understanding, risk taking, spontaneity, awareness, patience, integrity, independence, democracy, friendship, helping others.

Declaration: My core values represent who I am. My values, convictions, resolutions, beliefs and fears are held in my heart.

'And now, dear brother and sisters, one final thing. Fix your thoughts on what is true, and honourable, and right, and pure, and lovely, and admirable. Think about things that are excellent and worthy and praise.' (Philippians 4:8 NLT)

Action you can take—Dear me: Write a letter to your younger self. What advice would you give, for example, about forgiveness, valuing yourself, loving yourself, loving others, lessons learned? You can address the issues that mean the most to you.

Wise counsel: If we treated others the way we sometimes treat ourselves, questions would be asked. It's so easy to beat ourselves up. The Bible says that love is patient and kind. How easy is it for you to demonstrate those qualities to yourself? We can't change the past, but we can our future. Take your experiences, both good and bad, and learn from them.

'Love is patient and kind; love does not envy or boast; it is not arrogant or rude. It does not insist on its own way; it is not irritable or resentful; it does not rejoice at wrongdoing but rejoices with the truth. Love bears all things, believes all things, hopes all things, endures all things.' (1 Corinthians 13:4-7 ESV)

Action you can take—Love yourself: Spend a few hours at a shopping mall. Purposefully go into the high-end, expensive stores. Try on clothes, bags, shoes, jewellery etc. Before heading home, end the day with lunch and reflect on your experiences. How did this make you feel? On the way home, buy yourself a bouquet of flowers and a gift (it doesn't have to be expensive). The gift is for a later date, so must be sealed and opened within the next two weeks from the date of purchase. Aim to do this (whole experience) at least every two months.

Prayer point: Father, in the name of Jesus, I thank You that every good gift and every perfect gift comes from You. I choose to live every day with meaning and purpose. I know that wealth is not just about material items but, most importantly, love. Thank you for showing me how to value, love, and appreciate myself. Amen.

*'Thank you for making me so wonderfully complex! Your workmanship
is marvelous—how well I know it'* (Psalm 139:14 NLT).

Action you can take—Intervention: Set some time aside to research the
various interventions available—counselling, coaching, mentoring, or therapy.
Make a list of who does what? Which of these do you feel might help you to
move forward in life? Find out the cost, and within the next month, start saving
towards investing in some outside help.

Wise counsel: Internal healing is the starting point. Many people haven't
even considered working with a professional to help them on their path to
internal wellness. Long gone are the stigmas attached to these interventions.
People are tired of being tired; they are looking for solutions.

FAMILY

CHAPTER 5

Family

Sociologists define *family* as 'an intimate, domestic group of people related to one another by bonds of blood, sexual mating or legal ties, a resilient social unit adapted through time.'

Your definition may not look or sound the same, and that's OK. Truth be known, there are probably people you know who are not connected to you by blood or legal ties but have stuck closer to you than any brother or sister. Family is whatever it means to you, and that's what's important.

As a child, when you were growing up, your family was all you knew. Whatever 'dysfunction' may have been going on behind closed doors, you were either protected from it or you adapted to it; it became your 'normal'. As you've gotten older, you may have realised that what you experienced wasn't that normal after all. You now understand that there is no instruction manual for families other than the Word of God. Your parents may have brought you up based on the blueprint and traditions of their upbringing. It's very important to raise your awareness in this area so that you can break cycles of dysfunction and pain.

As basic as it sounds, it's important to remember that families are made up of people, and these people exhibit a variety of personality traits. Where there are people, there will be conflict and politics. You may have heard the adage that you cannot choose your family, so learning how to live with them is necessary. Learning is what may be needed in some cases.

We have a responsibility to lead by example and demonstrate the healthy qualities required to conceive a loving, loyal, protective environment, which every family needs. Good-quality family life must be intentional and cultivated. There must be forgiveness, acceptance, a respect for boundaries, and not least, unconditional love. If people need help, help them. If they need support, support them. If they need love, love them. And if they need forgiveness, forgive them. Choose to break toxic foundations and build new ones. Be the catalyst of change in your family. The aim of this chapter will help you to do that.

'A cheerful heart is good medicine, but a broken spirit saps a person's strength' (Proverbs 17:22 NLT).

Action you can take—Laugh: Invite family members over to your home for a 'comedy night' in. Watch funny movies, stand-up comedians, anything that will make you all laugh. The one rule is that every person must tell at least three jokes or impersonations. Make the day memorable by taking photographs. Arrange this at least twice a year.

Declare: I love to laugh, laughter brings healing. I have the joy of the Lord which is my strength.

'How good and pleasant it is when brothers live together in harmony!' (Psalm 133:1 CSB).

Action to take—A family fun day out: Organise a family and friends day out. What about a sports day or outing? Ideas could involve a theme park, zoo, museums, family picnic and so on. Ask around and gather a consensus. What would others like to do? Arrange this at least once a year.

Wise counsel: We often forget to schedule fun and recreation into our busy lives, work life balance brings harmony into life and is extremely important. The excitement and the laughter are the glue that keeps families together. This is living intentionally.

'The human body has many parts, but the many parts make up one whole body. So it is with the body of Christ' (1 Corinthians 12:12 NLT).

Action you can take—Embrace love languages: There are five love languages. Which of the following do you think applies to each member of your family? Which love language resonates with you the most?

- Gifts—Some people value receiving gifts. The cost doesn't matter to them; it's the thought that counts.
- Quality time—Some people value your full and undivided attention. They want to spend time with you.
- Physical touch—Some people love your physical presence. They love to give and receive hugs and cuddles.
- Acts of service—Some people like to be helped. They feel valued when they are assisted with bill paying, errands, and chores around the home.
- Words of affirmation—Some people feel valued when you pay them meaningful compliments.

Declare: Our unique make-up means that we don't give and receive love in the same way. I choose to be aware of this and do my part.

'Surely goodness and mercy shall follow me all the days of my life: and I will dwell in the house of the Lord for ever' (Psalm 23:6 KJV).

Action you can take—Legacy, fast forward: Within the next three months (from today's date), choose to do *two or all* of the following:

- Invite a family member, who you haven't contacted for longer than a month, over to your home.
- Visit a family member you have not seen for longer than two months.
- Call a family member you have not called for longer than two weeks.

Wise counsel: We must be purposeful and intentional about building and maintaining family relationships. How are you showing people in your family that you care about them? If love is a verb, what action are you taking?

'*Children are a gift from the Lord; they are a real blessing*'
(Psalm 127:3 GNT).

Action you can take—Come on over to my place: Arrange to spend a day with the children in your family. You could also invite the children of friends. Create an itinerary for the day consisting of a variety of activities, such as painting, colouring in, playing with play dough, putting puzzles together, watching cartoons, baking, telling stories, and having competitions. Lay on a small spread of children party foods. Aim to do this at the beginning and middle of each year.

Declare: I am intentional, and I choose to make the time to create magical memories for children.

'And he must be hospitable [to believers, as well as strangers], a lover of what is good, sensible (upright), fair, devout, self-disciplined [above reproach – whether in public or in private]' (Titus 1:8 AMP).

Action you can take—Sunday roast: Invite family members around for Sunday dinner. Make a day of it. Invite them each to prepare their favourite dish at your home. End the day with board and card games, movies, or other favourite fun activities. Host this a minimum of three times a year.

Prayer Point: Father, I thank You for Your presence in my home. Thank You for blessing me with a beautiful family. Thank You for teaching me to be hospitable and share my blessings with others. I am blessed to be a blessing. Amen.

'You will show me the way of life, granting me the joy of your presence and the pleasures of living with you forever'
(Psalm 16:11 NLT).

Action you can take: 'Celebrate good times, come on!' Plan and host a birthday brunch, meal, get-together, or party for yourself in the coming year. Start preparing now. Organise and arrange for a family portrait. Do you know the birthdays of everyone in your family? Put these dates in your diary and remember to send each person a suitable gesture, doesn't have to be a gift, a message or call should suffice.

Wise counsel: How do you feel when you receive a card or gift? It's not the expense of the gift, but the thought that somebody was thinking of you. A basic human need is to be loved and have a sense of belonging. Well done! You've just made somebody's day!

PERSONAL
DEVELOPMENT

CHAPTER 6

Personal Development

The reality is that we are where we are in life because of the choices we have made. My intention is not for you to feel bad, but for you to take stock of your current situation and take responsibility. You may have had a hard upbringing, and life may have dealt you some tough cards, but you cannot afford to allow that to defeat you.

Many women are walking around in a state of unconsciousness, completely unaware of how they got to where they currently are in life. I'm not, for one second, trivialising what you may have experienced. Rather, I am highlighting that you have a choice to stay within the parameters of your comfort zones. I will warn you though, this choice encourages you to become a victim of your circumstance. It takes a certain type of person to pursue the unknown. That person must be determined, irrespective of the obstacles that must be faced.

You can be who you want to be; with some exceptions, age should not be a barrier. Are you in a job that you resent? Are you sacrificing your purpose? What goals will positively impact your personal development during the next six months ? When your mind is being stretched and exposed to a higher level of learning, it's going to hurt. It's often at this stage that many of us stop and claim that learning isn't for us. This is when we need to find the resilience to push past the pain and remain focused. It's often easier to stay on course when you have a purpose—if you know your why.

If you don't do anything different in life, nothing changes. Every day is a gift, and tomorrow isn't guaranteed. Are you making the most of the time that has been allotted to you? Don't let your age, race, or level of education hold you back. Procrastination is fear disguised. Decide that you will be intentional about learning and growing for the rest of your life. Proverbs 18:16 says that people's gifts will make room for them and bring them before great people. Whether it's starting that degree, reading a book, or learning a new language, do something that will add value to you. This chapter will encourage you to cut the cords of mental limitation.

'Good planning and hard work lead to prosperity, but hasty shortcuts lead to poverty' (Proverbs 21:5 NLT).

Action you can take—Declaring goals: What are your goals? Goals need to be SMART: specific, measurable, attainable, relevant, and timed. They also must be personal to you.

- Write your goal down and place it somewhere visible.
- Set a realistic deadline—when would you like to achieve this goal?
- Break this goal into small segments. Which segment will you start with first?
- List everything and anything (doesn't matter how unrealistic it may seem) that you can do to achieve the goal.
- Prioritise your list. What is the first thing you should do? Continue prioritising and achieving as your list gets smaller.
- Work on each action point in the order of priority.
- Ensure that you do at least *one* action towards your goal every day. It doesn't matter how small it is. Keep doing this until you reach your goal.

Declare: Today I choose to make a start and take a step towards my designed life. I am confident and bold. I walk in alignment with my God-given gifts and talents. I am an overcomer.

'A wise man will hear, and will increase learning; and a man of understanding shall attain unto wise counsels' (Proverbs 1:5 KJV).

Action you can take—Improve your mind: Purchase three nonfictional books (audio books are great), within the next two months. Two of those books should be about topics you are passionate about. The other should be themed around personal development. Read (or listen to) one book for a minimum of one hour a day. Aim to finish one book per month.

Find an accountability partner, and share with him or her what you have learned.

Prayer Point: Father, in the name of Jesus, Your Word tells me that I can be transformed by the renewing of my mind. I tear down all lofty imaginings that exalt against what You say about me. Your Word says that through knowledge the just shall be delivered. I thank You for giving me the spirit of wisdom, knowledge, and understanding. I will study and show myself approved in all areas of my life and take the steps needed to move forward. Amen!

*'As iron sharpens iron, So one man sharpens [and influences]
another [through discussion]'* (Proverbs 27:17 AMP).

Action you can take—Stretch your development: Plan to invest a minimum of 2 per cent of your yearly income within the next twelve months on your personal development. What would you like to learn more about?

Within the next two weeks, starting from tomorrow, use an afternoon to search online for courses or seminars. Set out to attend or complete at *least* two courses or seminars per year (if you can do more, that's great!).

Wise counsel: You will not achieve anything if you remain in your comfort zone. Whatever you are expecting in life won't be found there. Your stretch zone is where you will be both challenged and motivated. This is the place where things happen. Fear is that dividing wall. The life you've always dreamed of is waiting for you. If you want something to change, *you* need to change something. Start small and build.

'To one he gave five talents, to another two talents, and to another one talent, depending on each one's ability' (Matthew 25:15 CSB).

Action you can take—Establish routine: For the next seven days, choose to go to bed one hour earlier than your normal bedtime, and wake up one hour earlier. Every day, follow these recommendations:

- Use 30 minutes a day for praise, worship, or prayer.
- Use 20 minutes a day for exercise.
- Use ten minutes a day for positive affirmations and mindfulness.

Declare: I dictate my day. I choose to be intentional with my time. Time is my most precious commodity.

'I can do all things through Christ which strengtheneth me' (Philippians 4:13 KJV).

Action you can take—Focus on completion: List all outstanding tasks, whether they pertain to you personally, at work, or at home. Design and create your own bespoke seven-day planner. Focus on completing *one* action point towards your overall tasks each day. It doesn't matter how small the action is. Do this until all tasks are complete. Ensure that you keep your planner somewhere visible.

Choose a way to celebrate once you have completed a task.

Prayer point: Father, in the name of Jesus, I have the authority to break and destroy every limitation in my mind. I thank You for the power of the blood. I've been given the authority to tear down all strongholds that have limited my progress. I speak things that are not as though they are. I am proactive and hardworking. I am consistent and committed. I will complete whatever I start. Amen.

'Study to shew thyself approved unto God, a workman that needeth not to be ashamed, rightly dividing the word of truth' (2 Timothy 2:15 KJV).

Action you can take—Increase profitability: Write down anything that could add value to your life. What could you do that you are not doing now? What could you do to increase your current skill set (people, leadership, customer service, business)? How valuable do you think you are to your current employer or the marketplace? Are you intentional in your current career? What do you need to do to change this if you are not? If you don't have a job, what can you do about your current situation?

Wise counsel: It's so easy to default into habit. It takes courage to look at where you are in life, irrespective of your age, and decide that you want change. Within a year from now, you could increase your value, and within three years, you could have a brand-new career. What's stopping you is you. It's time to raise the bar in this area and take control of where your life is going. Yes, it will feel hard at times. You may even want to give up. But I want you to imagine that gratifying feeling of completion! Against *all* odds, *you* did it!

'Where there is no vision, the people perish: but he that keepeth the law, happy is he' (Proverbs 29:18 KJV).

Action you can take—Analyse your time use: The aim of this exercise is to keep a record of how you spend your time. For the next three days, create a twenty-four-hour diary. Include the main things that you do such as eating, travelling, sleeping, watching TV, and so forth. On the fourth day, analyse your results and answer the following questions:

- What did you spend most of your time doing?
- How could you be more productive?
- How can you demonstrate that you have valued your time?
- What did you achieve?
- What can you do to manage your time more effectively?
- What could you do more or less of?

Keep in mind what success means to you, where you want to be, what your personal development needs are. Create a personal development plan for yourself. This is achieved by setting, reviewing, and revising goals when needed.

Declare: I have a plan and a purpose, which will propel me into my God given destiny.

CHAPTER 7

Finance

The way we perceive and manage money has a lot to do with our upbringing. Growing up constantly hearing 'we don't have enough money', living on welfare, or consistently struggling with money concerns could have had a negative impact on your relationship with financial concerns.

The consequences of your mindset will determine how much money you believe you are worth. If your self-perception is quite low, your perception of what you are worth in monetary terms will also be low.

Unconsciously, in your mind, you have set an amount that represents what you believe you are worth, and when you reach that limit you will stop. This will manifest in many ways. You will find yourself giving away your services for free, self-sabotaging, and squandering money, among other practices. If your mindset is not ready, a sudden shift from having no money to having vast amounts of it will impact your mental health quite negatively. In some cases, this can cause depression and anxiety.

Your mindset is one of the first things that you need to change if you want to change the amount of wealth you acquire. A vast majority of the world's population is living in poverty, or at least pay cheque to pay cheque, and they are burdened with debt. Many are living in bondage and are slaves to the lender (Proverbs 22). There is no shortcut to getting out of debt; it's going to take changing your mindset and habits.

Money is important; you can't do much of anything without it. The Bible says that the *love* of money is the root of all evil. Let's be clear—money isn't evil, and according to the Word of God does answer all things. You cannot live the life of abundance that God has called you to, or be in a position to bless others, if you don't have money. It's never too late to change and embrace the abundance mindset that says you can have and do anything concerning money. You just need to start. This chapter will help you think about your finances and raise your awareness of what financial freedom really is.

'Honor the Lord with your wealth and with the best part of everything you produce' (Proverb 3:9 NLT).

Action you can take—Give: Who are you committed to giving to? Give at *least* a tenth of your income to your church, an orphanage, a charity or a ministry.

Wise counsel: Where else are you taught that the more you give, the more you receive? Being a Kingdom citizen means you have Kingdom privileges. It's a God-given law that the more you sow, the more you reap. This does not only pertain to money. What else could you sow? It's good to be a cheerful giver. Continuously keep your motives in check. Remember that you don't give in order to receive. God gave the most precious gift to you—His son. Now that's giving!

'Go to the ant, thou sluggard; consider her ways, and be wise: Which having no guide, overseer, or ruler, Provideth her meat in the summer, and gathereth her food in the harvest. How long wilt thou sleep, O sluggard? When wilt thou arise out of the sleep? Yet a little sleep, a little slumber, a little folding of the hands to sleep: So shall thy poverty come as on that travelleth, and thy want as an armed man. (Proverbs 6:6-11 KJV)

Action you can take—Increase your income: How much do you need to be totally debt free? What is that significant *thing* you would like to save for (a car, a holiday, your mortgage, debt cancellation?). Create a plan by calculating the overall amount of money you need to achieve this goal. Now divide those years into months, and then break that down into weeks. How much will you need to save each month to get there? What could you do to increase your income and speed up this process? Work overtime? Get a second job? Sell items of furniture or clothing you no longer need?

Wise counsel: Discipline, commitment, and resilience are some of the qualities you must have before you can change any situation. You may need to make sacrifices and do things that you don't feel like doing at times. It's easier to persevere when you can envisage your goal clearly and are motivated by reminding yourself why you are doing it. Think of ways to increase your income to expedite your destination to financial freedom.

'And be not conformed to this world: but be ye transformed by the renewing of your mind, that ye may prove what is that good, and acceptable, and perfect, will of God' (Romans 12:2).

Action you can take—Improve your money mindset: Keep a journal in which you record your perception of money by answering the following questions:

- What money-related patterns did you see in your family when you were growing up?
- What bad examples did you experience about money when you were growing up?
- What good examples did you experience?
- What were you taught about investing?
- What were you taught about saving?
- What were you taught about paying bills?
- What does wealth mean to you?
- How has this impacted you today?

Declare: I am breaking negative financial cycles, perceptions, thought processes and a poverty mindset. My relationship with money is excellent. I am a wealth builder.

'*On the first day of every week, each one of you should set aside a sum of money in keeping with your income, saving it up*' (1 Corinthians 16:2 NIV).

Action—Save your pennies: Save £20 worth of £1 and £2 coins in a money jar every month. Save a minimum of £50 a month in a separate saving account. Save £50 per month towards an emergency fund (until it reaches a minimum of £1000). Save 1 per cent of your monthly earnings in a high-interest account.

Prayer Point: Father, in the name of Jesus, I am the head and not the tail. I will be the lender and not the borrower. My situation has already changed and will continue to change for the better. I have no doubt that I will always put Christ first and will always be encouraged that small changes can lead to big things. I am committed and will be consistently committed to being financially aware and a good steward.

*'Just as the rich rule the poor, so the borrower is
servant to the lender'* (Proverb 22:7 NLT).

Action you can take—Money management: List your income and your expenditures. Go through the last three months of bank statements. Colour code each item. For example, essentials such rent or mortgage could be yellow; food could be orange; travel, utilities, insurance, and all other essential expenses could be different colours. Now do the same for nonessentials. What spending patterns can you see? What have you learned from this? How can you improve on this? Get into the habit of doing this at least every month until you have a better understanding of your money.

Declare: I have great wisdom, knowledge, and understanding about wealth.

'Wisdom is supreme; therefore acquire wisdom. And whatever else you obtain, gain understanding' (Proverbs 4:7 BSB).

Action—Seek biblical finance advice: There are hundreds of Bible verses about finances. In the next thirty days find thirty Bible verses about finances, wealth, and prosperity. What is your understanding of what the word of God is saying?

Prayer Point: Father, in the name of Jesus, thank You for teaching me Your principles of how to be a good steward over my finances. Thank You for raising my awareness and restoring my hope. According to Jeremiah 29:11, the plans You have for me are to prosper me and not to harm me. They are plans to give me hope and a future. I am grateful that You wish above all things that I should prosper and be in health. Amen.

'*Invest in seven ventures, yes, in eight; you do not know what disaster may come upon the land*' (Ecclesiastes 11:2 NIV).

Action you can take—Practise purposeful investing: You are never too young or too old to start investing. Do your research and think about investing in any of the following: a retirement or pension plan, stocks, bonds, funds, individual saving accounts. If you're not a homeowner, you could explore the possibility of combining your finances with others (family members and friends) to buy a property. Speak to a financial planner about the best way to invest. Purchase blank gift cards from your favourite companies, top them up with any amount of your choice every month. Use it to treat yourself at the end of the year.

Find a free money-management app to download and use.

Wise counsel: Your Father in heaven wants you to prosper. We are where we are financially due to the decisions we have made. I encourage you to read the book of Proverbs, which is very much about wisdom. Make use of the information money managing experts present online. The first stage is being aware of where your money is going and changing your mindset. The next time you are out shopping, ask yourself, 'Do I need this or want this?' Your first impulsive response is your answer. If you don't need it, put it back and save towards it—or something much better—for another time.

CHAPTER 8

Home

Is there truly no place like home? Can you say this about your home? Does where you live reflect your personality and who you are? We are creatures of comfort, and our homes should be an intentional reflection of that. Love where you live, have pride, turn your house into a home. Whether you're living in a room, a flat on a council estate, or a detached house on a private road, love where you live.

Have you ever been to a house that looked undesirable on the outside, but inside could easily compete with any stately home? When God created the Garden of Eden, everything was intentional; every plant and creature had its unique colour, shape, and feature. The Bible says that God was pleased with everything that He had created. Everything He created was purposeful and had meaning. God's creatures are intentional about their habitats, whether it's a web, nest, or den. Just observe the intricate and purposeful detail that goes into the design of their homes.

Your home should matter because your environment has an impact on how you feel, so it's worth creating a positive one. Maintaining your home is important. God's instruction to Adam was to tend to the Garden of Eden, the upkeep of where we live is important.

What have you been putting off? If something is broken, fix it; if something is dirty, clean it; and if something is beyond repair, dispose of it. Beautiful homes don't just magically appear; they require intention and purpose.

Draw inspiration from nature and look around at the exquisite artistry on display. Nature is rich in its assortment of colours, shades, and textures. Makeovers don't need to be expensive; there are so many options out there, such as thrift and second-hand stores. You can renovate old items to transform your home. What about adding small items, such as throws, candles, cushions, and new handles. You'd be surprised what a difference room fragrances can make.

Coordinate, declutter, and rearrange your home. This doesn't cost any money, but it will bring a new, fresh energy to your personal environment. This chapter is aimed at exciting and awakening your creativity. It will hopefully encourage you to make the most of what you already have.

'To make artistic designs for work in gold, silver and bronze, to cut and set stones, to work in wood, and to engage in all kinds of crafts' (Exodus 31:4–5 NIV).

Action you can take—Pay attention to the details: Imagine that an interior designer has been invited to your home. Choose a room in your current home that you would like to transform. Answer the following questions:

- What do you love about this room?
- What do you dislike in this room?
- What colours do you love?
- What mood are you trying to achieve?
- What was the last thing you did to this room?
- What can you do to improve this room?

Create a vision board for this room, and others if you want to. Include pictures along with swatches of colours and textures.

Declare: My home is my sanctuary. I am intentional and purposeful about my surroundings.

He has filled them with skill to do every sort of work done by an engraver or by a designer or by an embroiderer in blue and purple and scarlet yarns and fine twined linen, or by a weaver—by any sort of workman or skilled designer. (Exodus 35:35 ESV)

Action you can take—Embrace your DIY creativity: Minor touches of creativity can literally transform your home. Look around your home to see what can be implemented.

Gather some inspiration from magazines, websites, show homes, and exhibitions. Get out your paints and glue guns. Here are some ideas:

- Add some faux or real plants.
- Organise drawers with storage inserts.
- Cover pieces of medium-density fibreboard (MDF) with samples of beautiful wallpaper or fabric to create centrepieces and features.
- Reupholster tired furniture. Add beads, diamantes, or buttons.
- Incorporate different textures like faux furs and leathers with throws and cushions.
- Create the illusion of space with large mirrors.
- Use pale, neutral colours for a peaceful atmosphere.
- Reinvent old photo frames, lamp shades, boxes, jars, clocks, handles, and so forth.

Prayer Point: Father, in the name of Jesus, You are the ultimate creator and designer. I am creative and have the spirit of excellence just like You. Thank You for giving me imagination. I draw my inspiration from Your creation in nature. Amen.

*'But if one does not know how to manage the own household,
how will he care for the church of God?'* (1 Timothy 3:5 BSB).

Action you can take—#deepclean #declutter: It's time to spring clean—or 'deep' clean. Create a plan of what needs to be cleaned in each room. Include tidying and cleaning all storage cabinets, cupboards and drawers. Include your fridge and pantry. Sanitise dustbins, toilets, handles, doorknobs, and other frequently trafficked areas. Wash all skirting boards, internal doors, windows, and window frames. Clean mirrors and glass. Dust and polish shelves and all storage areas. Deep steam-clean mattresses and turn them over. Declutter and reorganise kitchen cupboards and bathroom cabinets. Dust and polish surfaces. Vacuum curtains, blinds, and sofas. Re-plump cushions. Finish by adding a beautiful air freshener to each room. Do this once a month.

Wise counsel: You'd be surprised what impact a clean and clutter-free home will have on your mental state. Make a decision to not let 'things' accumulate, collecting clutter and ultimately chaos. How you live reflects who you are. God is a God of principles. Do not despise humble beginnings. Make the best of what you have. He will then elevate you to the next level.

Moreover there are workmen with thee in abundance, hewers and workers of stone and timber, and all manner of cunning men for every manner of work. Of the gold, the silver, and the brass, and the iron, there is no number. (1 Chronicles 22:15–16 KJV)

Action you can take—Food, glorious food: Cooking should be pleasurable. Each month, invest a bit of your income until your kitchen is well stocked with: sharp chef knives, chopping boards, food processor, spatulas, mixing bowls, pastry brushes, colanders, strainers, scoops, tongs, whisks, potato peelers, serving bowls, Pyrex dishes, mallets, measuring containers, ramekins, scales, rolling pin, muffin tin, sheet pan, biscuit cutter, garlic presser, icing bag, sharpening stone, pots, pans, serving dishes, along with everyday crockery, mugs, special-occasion crockery and glassware, table mats, coasters, and an assortment of glass jars.

What do you need to throw out or add to?

Wise counsel: Having the right resources and equipment will make life easier, not only in the kitchen but in every area of your life. Why struggle and make do when you don't have to? Take inventory of where you currently are, set a goal of where you want to be. Invest and take action to get there.

'I made me gardens and orchards, and I planted trees in them of all kind of fruits. I made me pools of water, to water therewith the wood that bringeth forth trees' (Ecclesiastes 2:5–6 KJV)

Action you can take—Adopt some nature: Have you thought about introducing more plants and flowers into your home? What changes can you make in your garden? Consult some gardening magazines for inspiration on various types of flowers, plants, trees, garden ornaments, water features, and garden furniture.

Declare: Surrounding myself with the beauty of nature makes me feel so happy.

Then Jesus said, 'Come to me, all of you who are weary and carry heavy burdens, and I will give you rest. Take my yoke upon you. Let me teach you, because I am humble and gentle at heart, and you will find rest for your souls. For my yoke is easy to bear, and the burden I give you is light.' (Matthew 11:28–30 NLT)

Action you can take—Make space for R & R: Dedicate a space or a room in your home as your 'relaxation zone'. What items could you put there to create an area of peace, tranquillity, and mindfulness? What about a comfy chair or luxurious oversized cushions, scented candles, mood lamps, a comfy footstool, a bookshelf?

Prayer Point: Father in the name of Jesus, teach me the power of rest. You rested on the seventh day. Teach me how to relax, be still, and know that You are God. You are the Prince of peace, the peace that surpasses all understanding. Amen.

'But as for me and my house, we will serve the Lord'
(Joshua 24:15 KJV).

Action you can take—Create memorabilia: Create a photo album specifically for your home. Take photos of each room and write a brief positive statement or memory about it. Include the dates and times. In years to come, this will be of great sentimental value.

Write an appreciation list of all the things relating to your home that you are grateful for.

Declare: Father, as I abide in You, I take comfort knowing that You abide in me. My home is Your home.

CHAPTER 9

Health

If we feel pain in our bodies, we consult a doctor. Often these are tangible and visible signs of something wrong. But what happens if we feel depressed or low for a longer period than what is deemed 'normal'? What usually happens is nothing; we just get on with life. We frighteningly overlook the condition of our mental health so easily.

Did you know that serotonin—the hormone that our bodies produce that makes us feel happy—is produced in your gut? It shares the same tissue as your brain. It stands to reason that a deficiency in vital minerals and vitamins will inevitably impact your mood. I do believe that what we eat plays a very important part of our mental well-being.

There are many women who don't feel good about their bodies, and they often reach for those 'bad foods', because they release dopamine, which provides instant gratification. These foods ultimately perpetuate weight gain, which, in turn, impacts our moods and often leaves us feeling bloated, deflated, and defeated. It's a vicious cycle, it's time to get off the hamster wheel.

As enticing and convenient as processed foods are, we cannot ignore the fact that they are loaded with chemicals and hydrogenated fats. These foods are addictive, and when eaten excessively almost certainly play a part in our declining health, including heart disease, high blood pressure, and diabetes amongst other conditions.

Did you know that drinking water is a vital part of your diet? Not only because 60 per cent of your body is made up of it, but because it's also crucial for flushing out toxins from your liver, aiding digestion, and improving brain function amongst other great benefits.

It is a known fact that foods rich in vitamin B help produce serotonin. At the beginning of creation, God gave us some great advice. He told us that He had given us every herb bearing seed and fruit to eat (Genesis 1:29). If God Himself said it, there must be something in it. I believe this is the key to a healthy body and mind.

'Do you not know that your bodies are temples of the Holy Spirit, who is in you, whom you have received from God? You are not your own' (1 Corinthians 6:19 NIV).

Action you can take—Schedule medical check-ups: When was the last time you made an appointment with your:

- GP
- Dentist
- Optician

Do you know whether you are within the correct BMI range? Is your blood pressure within the healthy remit? What about your cholesterol? Have you had that checked recently? Have you had a diabetes and a smear test? Book all outstanding appointments within the next month.

Wise counsel: How will you know what you need to do more of, or eat less of, unless you know exactly where you are regarding your health? We often bury our heads in the sand and allow things to deteriorate. We need to be as diligent with our bodies as we are about servicing our cars. If you continue driving a car without oil, it will eventually seize up and break down. Prevention is better than cure. Please look after yourself before it's too late.

'She is energetic and strong, a hard worker' (Proverbs 31:17 NLT).

Action you can take—Get moving: Start this on a Monday. For the next five days, choose one of the following exercises to do for 15 minutes a day:

- **Cardio**—Jogging, running in place, jumping jacks, squats, skipping, jumping in place (anything that raises your heart rate!).
- **Exercises for arms, legs, buttocks, stomach**—You can find all sorts of exercises online. Follow the instructions carefully.

On the following Monday, increase the types of exercises you do and the amount of time to exercise by five minutes. Continue the process until you are exercising for sixty minutes per day. Once you have achieved this, reduce the number of days to three per week. (Of course, if you would like to do more, all the better!)

Wise counsel: Thinking of exercise as unpleasant is often the reason we find it so hard to start. Focus on the result. What are you hoping to achieve and gain? Exercising in small, bite-sized, manageable segments of time will make the journey achievable. Doing a little of something each day will amount to big changes overall. It's time to bring your sexy back. Have patience; you will soon see results!

'If you lie down, you will not be afraid; when you lie down, your sleep will be sweet' (Proverbs 3:24 ESV).

Action you can take—Get some sleep: For the next three nights, ensure that you get at least seven to nine hours of sleep.

Here are some tips for those who find it hard to sleep:

- Soak in a warm bath and follow it with a warm drink.
- Massage your head and feet.
- Use a herbal medication which helps aid sleep.
- Put your phone away an hour before bedtime.
- Exercise at least an hour before bed.
- Meditate and pray.
- Establish a set routine before bedtime. (Studies have shown that this subconsciously tells your mind to shut down and slowdown in preparation for rest.)

What other ideas can you think of?

If you actively use social media, for the next seven days, measure just how much time you have spent on it. For the following seven days, limit your usage on all social media platforms to just one hour a day. Do this at least twice a month.

Declare: I invite deep, soul-nourishing, contented, well-deserved rest to my soul.

'Cast all your anxiety on Him, because He cares for you' (1 Peter 5:7).

Action you can take—Practise mindfulness: For the next 21 days, find a peaceful quiet environment and set at least 15 to 30 minutes aside. You can choose to sit in silence or play some instrumental worship music in the background. Meditate on just how much your Heavenly Father adores and loves you. Use the last five minutes to give thanks.

Prayer Point: Father, in the name of Jesus, I know that I am loved by You. I am comforted and reminded in Your Word, that tells me not to worry about anything. If You care for the birds of the air, and clothe the lilies of the field, how much more will You do for me? I am comforted to know that I can cast my burdens onto You. Thank You, that You will give me rest when I am heavy laden, because Your yoke is easy and Your burden is light. Amen.

'Do not join those who drink too much wine or gorge themselves on meat' (Proverb 23:20 BSB).

Challenge—Be aware of your eating habits: You can do this alone or in a group. It's time to think about your eating patterns. Take some time to answer these questions:

In which of the following situations do you find yourself emotionally eating:
- When you are anxious?
- When you are bored?
- When you are stressed?
- When you are sad?
- When you are working?

What emotional void is the substitution of food trying to fill? Do you eat only when you are hungry? What trends or patterns can you see with your relationship with food? What will you change as you move forward?

Create a seven-day *healthy* eating plan for breakfast, lunch, dinner, and snacks. Choose two of those days to be meat free. Include drinking at least eight glasses of water a day. Significantly reduce your salt and sugar intake. Eat as many fruits and vegetables as you like. Do this at least once a month.

Wise counsel: Raising your awareness and understanding why you eat the way you do is vital. Many of us eat when we are emotionally charged and will often use food as a form of comfort. We form patterns of eating over time, even from childhood. Are you always conscious of the nutritional value you are adding to your body when you eat? Many sicknesses derive from our diets, and in contrast, many have been healed as a result of their consumption. Your relationship with food starts in your mind.

'*We are destroying sophisticated arguments and every exalted and proud thing that sets itself up against the [true] knowledge of God, and we are taking every thought and purpose captive to the obedience of Christ.*' (2 Corinthians 10:5 AMP)

Action you can take—Seek health advice in the Word: Find ten inspirational Bible verses that relate to a healthy mind or body. What did you learn from each verse?

Declare: I choose to feast on the Word of God. It's His report that I believe.

'All discipline for the moment seems not to be joyful, but sorrowful;
yet to those who have been trained by it, afterwards it yields
the peaceful fruit of righteousness.' (Hebrews 12:11 NASB)

Action you can take—Be accountable with your diet: List ten reasons *each* why the excessive consumption of sugar, salt, and white flour can be damaging to your health.

What have you learned from this exercise? What will you do differently from today?

Declaration: I am disciplined and ready for a change. I am aware and intentional about my food habits. When I look good, I feel good.

AFFIRMATIONS

(Reminder—without God, we are none of these.)

Say these whilst looking in the mirror twice a day!

I am a child of God!

I am a person of value; I am precious. My worth is far above the value of rubies.

I am the righteousness of God.

I am focused and driven.

I am balanced and fair.

I am considerate and kind.

I am an overcomer—more than a conqueror!

I am powerful, wealthy, rich, and resourceful.

I am innovative and creative.

I exude much wisdom, knowledge, and understanding.

I am loved, lovable, and loving.

I am bold, confident, and assertive.

I am complete and whole.

I am the head and not the tail, above and not beneath.

I am fearfully and wonderfully made.

Printed in the United States
By Bookmasters